CAREERS IN

Internet Advertising and Marketing

JEANNE NAGLE

ROSEN
PUBLISHING
NEW YORK

Published in 2014 by The Rosen Publishing Group, Inc.
29 East 21st Street, New York, NY 10010

Library of Congress Cataloging-in-Publication Data

Nagle, Jeanne.
Careers in Internet advertising and marketing/Jeanne Nagle.—First
edition.
     pages cm.—(Careers in computer technology)
Includes bibliographical references and index.
ISBN 978-1-4488-9596-0 (library binding)
1. Marketing—Vocational guidance. 2. Computer science—Vocational
guidance. 3. Internet marketing. 4. Internet advertising. I. Title.
HF5415.35.N34 2014
381'.142023—dc23

                                                                2012043445

Manufactured in the United States of America

CPSIA Compliance Information: Batch #S13YA: For further information, contact Rosen Publishing, New York, New York, at
1-800-237-9932.

Contents

Marketing and advertising are two important means by which companies are able to sell their goods and services. Yet these tools of the sales trade are effective only if the target audience—made up of consumers who are most likely to make a particular type of purchase—receives the messages that marketers and advertisers are sending. Therefore, the message a seller creates is important, but so are the media, meaning the various forms of communication, used to get that message across.

For centuries people and companies have used whatever means available to get the word out about themselves and their products or services. At first, there was word of mouth, where customers told their friends and neighbors about purchases that satisfied them. Posting flyers announcing items for sale or events worked well at one point, as did placing ads and notices in print media, such as newspapers and magazines. Radio and television have served as electronic marketing and advertising tools for years.

These days companies are turning to the Internet as another source of message delivery. From simply surfing the Net for entertainment purposes to flexing their buying muscle with online purchases, more and more people around the world are using the Internet and becoming Web savvy. According to the Web site Internet World

This Internet advertisement promotes an online sweepstakes. It is sponsored by NEC America, appearing on the side of the Yahoo! financial advice page.

Stats, Internet use around the world rose more than 500 percent in the first decade of the twenty-first century, and it doesn't show signs of stopping. A company's best chance of reaching all these possible customers who are online would be to market themselves on the Internet. Many companies are realizing this and are doing something about it. According to a quarterly report by the Nielsen research group, spending on Internet ads is on the rise, outpacing money spent on any other form of media.

An increase in Internet advertising and marketing is good news for anyone interested in working in these areas. After all, greater demand means more job openings for people who can run marketing campaigns and create online ads. There are several different positions available in these fields, each with a specific set of duties. Just a few examples include overseeing an entire marketing department as a top executive, or director; working directly with customers to market their goods as an account manager; finding just the right words and pictures that will attract customers as a copywriter or graphic designer; analyzing data and measuring the success of marketing efforts as a search engine optimization specialist; and strategizing where and in what formats a marketing message should appear, then securing that space, as an online media specialist.

These and several more interesting careers await eager applicants in the exciting world of Internet advertising and marketing. In the following sections, readers will find insight into the duties, educational requirements, and future hiring prospects for several of the most popular and challenging careers in these fields.

A t their very heart, marketing and advertising are about communication. Because they have virtually the same goals and use some similar methods, marketing and advertising are often thought of as the same thing. There are differences between the fields, though, which make them two distinct career paths. This section examines how marketing and advertising are defined, how they are similar and different, and how Internet (or digital) marketing and advertising differ from traditional forms of these fields. Along the way readers will also learn about general marketing processes, strategies, and terms.

THE ROLE OF MARKETING

The American Marketing Association defines marketing as "the activity, set of institutions, and processes for creating, communicating, delivering, and exchanging offerings that have value for customers, clients, partners, and society at large." Perhaps a simpler way to think of marketing is to consider the root of the word itself. The main goal of marketing is to bring something to market so that it can be bought and sold.

The concept behind marketing as a career, however, is more involved than that. Marketing is an entire series of actions that, if completed properly, helps companies establish a good working relationship with both current and potential

Patrons enjoy beverages outside a Starbucks in Lisbon, Portugal. Clever, focused marketing has made Starbucks a worldwide name brand that, in the minds of many, is synonymous with coffee.

customers. When customers feel good about a company or individual, they are more likely to do business with that company or person. That translates to sales. Therefore, marketing seeks to make and strengthen connections between a company and its customers through familiarity.

When customers recognize a product or company as their favorite, chances are good that they will continue to buy that particular product from that company, even if they need to pay more for it. This is what's known in marketing as brand loyalty. Many marketing techniques are centered on building

BRANDING

In the Old West, cowboys used to brand their cattle, literally burning their mark on the herd as a way to identify them indelibly as theirs. Today, businesses participate in branding of a different type, using marketing techniques to claim products and services as their own in the minds of customers.

A business's name, logo, and catchphrase—all things that help customers identify a company and set it apart from others—are only a part of branding. In a way, a brand is like a company's personality, and it takes many elements into consideration. A person's history, actions, words, and associations all help shape his or her personality.

The same is true of a company brand. Marketers build a brand by promoting, or calling attention to, a company's past successes, good deeds done to benefit individuals or entire communities, promises made and kept, and the people associated with the company, whether it's a CEO, employees who deal with customers on an everyday basis, or celebrities who appear in commercials for a product or product line.

brand loyalty by presenting companies as trusted "friends" who provide quality and value.

The environment in which marketing professionals work can vary greatly. Marketing departments can be found in many different types of companies, where the marketing function is performed in-house (directly within the company). Marketing also is performed by stand-alone businesses, referred to as marketing firms.

OUTBOUND AND INBOUND MARKETING

There are two types of marketing, namely outbound and inbound. Outbound marketing is the more traditional of the two. Before the arrival of the Internet, salespeople had to reach out to find customers by sending out sales messages to the general public in the hope that many people would respond. The responses they were looking for were sales. Typical outbound marketing techniques include cold calling, or making sales calls to people who are not customers and may not have expressed an interest in buying the product being sold. Techniques also include mailing out letters and pamphlets to prospective clients, and print and broadcast advertising.

Outbound marketing techniques are still used, of course, even in digital advertising and marketing. E-mail sales messages are the electronic equivalent of direct mail, and plenty of advertisements appear along the top and sides of Web pages, or pop up as users download the latest music or

YouTube video. But more and more, marketers are turning to inbound marketing methods in order to make sales. Rather than sending out messages, inbound marketing revolves around creating marketing materials that Internet users will find in searches they create themselves.

THE ROLE OF ADVERTISING

Advertising is an arm, or a branch, of marketing. Whereas marketing is concerned with creating a good feeling about a company as a producer of many things, advertising narrows the focus to raising awareness of a specific product or line of products. Advertising is a more direct manner of selling, where a product's value, specialness, and advantages over

Advertisements for sunglasses and clothing flank a social networking page. Online ads of this type are considered part of outbound marketing campaigns.

other similar products are highlighted in an attempt to convince customers that the item is worth buying.

Advertising jobs are typically performed by workers in companies that specialize in advertising. These advertising firms are companies in their own right, not simply a department of a larger company.

TRADITIONAL AND DIGITAL

There are differences between traditional and digital forms of advertising and marketing. As mentioned in the introduction, the primary difference is the type of media in which the work is done. Yet there's more to it than that.

Marketing experts have compared traditional marketing to a one-sided, or one-way, conversation. All communication comes from one source—the client and/or whomever the client has hired to do the company's marketing—and is given to the prospective customer. In this scenario, the marketer or advertiser does all the talking. The only say the customer has in the matter is whether or not to accept the message he or she is receiving and act on it.

Digital marketing, on the other hand, is a two-way street that involves communicating back and forth between the marketer/advertiser and the customer. There's still information coming from clients via their marketing or advertising teams, but the media through which the message is delivered are digital, which by its nature makes the marketing interactive. With digital marketing, customers are invited and even encouraged to respond almost immediately by clicking on a link, responding to a social networking post, or otherwise engaging with the source.

Online marketing and advertising jobs require teamwork, where each individual plays a role in creating the finished product.

Yet for all their differences, traditional and digital advertising and marketing are, in some ways, simply two sides of the same coin. A combination of investigating, planning, creating, and communicating goes into any campaign, which is what individual advertising and marketing projects are called. Hard work is put in by dedicated marketing and advertising professionals, whether they are working offline or online.

Many of the jobs in digital advertising and marketing that are discussed here will be similar to jobs that are available in the traditional versions of these fields. The general categories or overarching disciplines will be the same, the titles will be almost identical, and the job duties will be pretty comparable. The major difference will be in the media or format, which is digital.

CHAPTER 2

Digital Directors and Account Managers

There is a hierarchy, meaning an order or ranking by status, attached to many jobs, but this is particularly true in marketing and advertising. At the top are the executives, who are the directors and managers. These people oversee the work of others and often take the lead on various projects themselves.

ONLINE MARKETING DIRECTOR

Marketing directors are the people in charge of all activity within a company's marketing department or as the head of an individual marketing firm. Therefore, an online marketing director would be the person who oversees every aspect of all the company's Internet-related marketing efforts combined.

The advertising departments of most companies are led by the marketing director. Within an advertising agency, however, there exists a level of upper management that may contain a director, who would be the top boss. Since "interactive advertising"—advertising that uses the Internet and digital media—has become a separate department in many advertising agencies, it is safe to assume that there are a fair number of directors who oversee Internet advertising specifically. The roles for both a marketing director and the director of an advertising agency are virtually identical. Therefore, in

Developing plans and making sure information is shared with all members of the marketing team are the responsibility of online marketing directors.

this section, the term "online marketing director" will be used to cover both the online marketing and online advertising manager positions.

WHAT THEY DO

In many ways, the online marketing director is the mastermind of all Internet marketing operations, which means the actions that let a business or department function smoothly and, it is hoped, be successful. Planning is a big part of what online marketing directors do. They are in charge of figuring out how to bring in new customers and keep old ones. That requires strategic thinking and developing a plan of action, or simply, a marketing plan. Marketing plans detail goals that marketing efforts are expected to achieve and list specific ways to reach those goals. Marketing directors are responsible not only for developing a business plan, and making any needed changes as the situation warrants, but for making sure the plan is followed as well.

Online marketing directors are decision makers who help guide the direction of their department's or company's Internet marketing efforts. Some of the ways in which they accomplish this are by hiring and overseeing marketing professionals who are talented at their jobs, making sure their employees have the latest equipment and training, and keeping current on trends in the field. They work closely and cooperatively with other departments involved in their company's Internet marketing initiatives, particularly information technology employees, to develop a good working relationship and make sure important information is shared. Online marketing directors are also responsible for their department or company budgets, as well as writing reports that detail what is happening within their department and how successful those efforts have been. Some online marketing directors also have a hand in the actual marketing process, from creative work like copywriting to dealing directly with customers and developing new products.

EDUCATION AND TRAINING NEEDED

People who would like to become online marketing directors would do well to study business and communications in school. In high school, that might translate into math and

Receiving computer training while in high school is an important step for anyone seeking a career in Internet marketing.

English courses. Because they will be dealing quite a bit with technology and the Internet, future online marketing directors also might want to receive some kind of computer training. Of course, computer programming classes and writing code would not be necessary, but understanding how Internet search engines work and learning how to operate the most current software programs could be invaluable.

Joining (or starting, if necessary) an entrepreneurs club or a debate/speech team is also a good idea. These organizations teach how to work with others and communicate effectively. Junior Achievement is a national organization that provides excellent experience in running a business, including how

ADVICE FROM AN ONLINE MARKETING DIRECTOR

As the owner of her own marketing firm that specializes in social media and brand strategy, Jeneane assumes the role of online marketing director. She supervises the work of four content specialists who work for her. On any given day she can be found participating in brainstorming sessions with clients and her employees, supervising the development of blogs and Web sites, and writing content herself for clients. "My primary duties in all of this are discerning what marketing solution best fits with a client's business objectives, then developing a plan to develop that solution," she says. "I align the online/social and traditional communications vehicles accordingly, develop tasks and timelines, and then assign resources as needed."

As someone who hires others to work in online marketing, Jeneane has some pertinent advice for anyone looking to enter the field. "Read blogs as often as you can to keep the pulse of the market. Participate on Twitter and LinkedIn at a minimum, and build your social circle and social capital. Don't just read, but participate. Know your market and interact with them accordingly online. If you have a personal blog, consider starting a more professional blog. You should have multiple outlets for multiple purposes. If you can attend conferences—online or in person—do so. Webinars, professional events, and marketing conferences are important and powerful ways to learn the latest trends and arm yourself professionally, but also give you valuable information that you can then share with others.

"Finally, hone your critical-thinking skills. Your ability to think, discern, interpret, and communicate are very valuable skills that seem to be in short supply. These items can be demonstrated through your own participation online—through the things you read, the knowledge/humor/gifts you share, the online spheres you participate in, the events you attend, and the unique understanding you bring to the job."

to market products and services. Another advantage of participating in some kind of business-centered extracurricular activity is that it looks good on a résumé and shows that the participant is serious about his or her career choices.

As far as most companies are concerned, a bachelor's degree is the minimum educational requirement for employment in the marketing field, especially when it comes to management and director positions. Bachelor's degree programs in business or marketing typically include courses in business writing, finance, promotions, managerial techniques, salesmanship, and communications. Some colleges and universities even offer programs that specialize in Internet marketing. Many companies prefer that their executives hold an advanced degree, such as a master's of business administration (MBA).

WHAT THE FUTURE HOLDS

According to the U.S. Bureau of Labor Statistics's *Occupational Outlook Handbook*, the need for marketing managers and directors of all types is expected to be strong. This should be particularly true for online marketing directors because of the continued growth of the Internet as a medium for marketing and advertising campaigns.

Experience counts when trying to get any executive position. Many times directors are hired from within, meaning people with nonmanagerial positions already working for a company are promoted to managerial status. Someone just starting out in the marketing field may very well have to start from the bottom up, or "pay dues" by working in another capacity, before earning a spot as an online marketing director.

ONLINE MARKETING ACCOUNT MANAGER

It takes an entire team of people to take an online marketing campaign from start to successful completion. Yet except for the marketing manager/director, the only team member the client usually sees on a regular basis is the account manager. Because they work so closely with clients, account managers can be considered the face of a company's digital marketing department. These professionals are the relationship builders of an online marketing team.

The job of online marketing account managers is to be the contact person for clients, outside vendors, and team members throughout a campaign.

WHAT THEY DO

In general, online marketing managers put into motion and run marketing plans they've designed to create more sales for each of their clients. The most important duties of these marketing professionals revolve around client relations. Obviously, the more client accounts there are, the more money there is to be made by marketing firms and departments. Therefore, it is in the best interest of an online marketing account manager to cultivate new clients and keep current clients happy.

Using their excellent people skills, online marketing account managers make clients feel special, secure in their business decisions, and above all, satisfied with the results of their marketing campaign. Online marketing managers listen carefully to their clients' needs and respond to those needs in a timely and effective manner. These marketing professionals work out of an office, but travel may be required to meet with some clients.

Whereas an online marketing director oversees all marketing efforts within his or her company, department, or territory, an online account manager is responsible for all marketing initiatives performed for individual clients. Each client has an account, or a business agreement, wherein a marketing firm or department promises, for a fee, to provide services designed to promote the client and bring in sales. Online marketing account managers handle the digital and new media end of a client's account.

In order to find what methods would work best for a particular client, the online marketing account manager must gather data and analyze it thoroughly, making decisions about the direction an account should take based on his or her findings. Sources for this kind of research include reading trade publications (magazines and newspapers that publish stories concerning a client's particular field) and conducting surveys. Another avenue for information gathering involves performing what's known as Web analytics, which is information on how and why the public uses a client's Web site. Online marketing account managers need to either work with a Web analytics expert or perform at least a simplified version of this tactic on their own to get this vital information.

Online marketing account managers also do their homework regarding the performance of the marketing work being done for their clients. They compile sales information, write reports, and give presentations based on those reports, with either the client or their company's marketing executives, or both, as their audience.

EDUCATION AND TRAINING NEEDED

Communication and interpersonal skills are the two of the strongest tools of an online marketing account manager's trade. Taking courses and receiving other types of training in these areas should be the top priority for anyone wishing to make a career for him- or herself in this field. Courses in communications and business would be ideal. Those whose high schools don't offer classes such as these can still benefit from the standard English and math curriculum offered by all schools. Electives such as creative writing, speech, economics, psychology, sociology, and design should be considered for inclusion in a future account manager's course load.

A sequence of classes in at least one foreign language could prove very useful. Marketing on the Internet is capable

Presenting a report in front of classmates demonstrates written, verbal, planning, and interpersonal skills. Online account managers have to be proficient in all these areas and more.

of reaching millions of people worldwide, not all of whom speak or read English. Being able to provide Web site text in more than one language is a smart business move. Also, some online marketing account managers deal with international clients. Being able to communicate with them in their native language is convenient and also a sign of respect for the client's culture.

To obtain a job in marketing, especially at the management level, a person should have at least a bachelor's degree, preferably in marketing, advertising, or business. College courses are generally pretty expansive, so students should be able to sign up for more field-specific classes as an under-grad than they were able to in high school. Depending on the college they attend, students may even be able to major or minor in digital marketing. An MBA or another advanced degree, perhaps in marketing itself, is looked upon favorably by employers for a position such as this.

WHAT THE FUTURE HOLDS

The future looks bright for marketing account managers of all stripes, particularly for those who concentrate on digital marketing. A number of sources, including the *Occupational Outlook Handbook* and Canada's National Occupational Classification (NOC), predict that marketing manager positions should be available for many years. As the competition for making sales continues to increase, companies will look for ways to gain an edge. One of those ways should be to hire online marketing managers, which means that these positions should be on the upswing as well.

ONLINE ADVERTISING ACCOUNT EXECUTIVE

Advertising agencies and advertising departments of companies or marketing firms are the locations where online advertising account executives can be found. Much like online marketing managers, who are their counterparts in the marketing world, online advertising account representatives interact quite a bit with clients to design campaigns that increase sales of the client's product or services. The difference between the two positions is that advertising account execs concentrate on a product or product line. Marketing account managers focus on the bigger picture of "selling" a company brand. Furthermore, the difference between an online advertising account executive and a traditional advertising account exec is, of course, that the online position deals with digital advertising and new media.

WHAT THEY DO

Guiding digital advertising campaigns for individual products from start to finish is the job of online advertising account

When scanned, QR codes link viewers to online content that is developed by online advertising account professionals.

executives. Online advertising account executives are the workers in charge of overseeing the production of online banner ads, the digital content that viewers see when they click on a link or scan a QR code, and more.

Online advertising account executives coordinate the work of many individuals. People in this field act as liaisons between the client and the rest of the online advertising department, particularly the creative and production people who make a concept into an actual advertisement. More than simply acting as a go-between, online advertising execs also participate in the creation of campaigns by offering their insight into the marketplace and contributing creative ideas.

Creating digital advertising campaigns starts with strategy. Online advertising account executives conduct research into the products their clients are trying to sell, as well as how similar products are selling in various markets. Based on his or her findings, the advertising exec then comes up with a plan regarding how to present the client's product online in a way that delivers the best result, meaning increased sales.

Once the plan is in place, the online advertising account executive tracks the progress of work done on the campaign by other members of the team, making sure that the job comes in on time and on budget. He or she also keeps tabs on the effectiveness of any online advertising done on behalf of the client once it appears on the Internet. Writing and presenting reports to share the findings of any research with clients and others in the advertising agency or firm are also part of an online advertising executive's job.

EDUCATION AND TRAINING

While in high school, individuals who would like to pursue a career as an online advertising account executive should pay special attention to classes in English, social studies, computer science, and economics. As mentioned, advertising and marketing firms prefer that their employees have a college degree. Moving on to college, students would benefit from majoring in marketing, business, or, if available, advertising. Another point to remember regarding a college degree in

Major multinational advertising agencies, such as Publicis, offer internships to help recent high school and college graduates get started in the industry.

this field is that when it comes to getting a job, having a bachelor's degree is good and an advanced degree is even better.

Beyond studying these disciplines, college students can get real-world experience by seeking out an internship at an advertising agency. Interns may mostly do administrative work, at least at first, but any agency experience allows students to see firsthand what their work life would be like.

WHAT THE FUTURE HOLDS

The U.S. Department of Labor forecasts that advertising account executive jobs, online or not, will be available for years to come. However, competition for these positions is expected to be fierce. Advertising agencies are expected to continue to be the top employers of online advertising account executives, although companies in other industries that create their own advertising campaigns should also be hiring. Several employment sources indicate that those individuals who do secure a position as an online account executive should expect to receive a salary in the high to mid five figures to the low six figures.

It takes an entire team to run a successful online advertising or marketing campaign. Yet it's a pretty safe bet that when they think of advertising, most people automatically associate writers and designers with the term. That's because the text, especially catchphrases, and overall look of an ad or marketing piece are the most familiar to the public. If account managers are to clients the face of online campaigns, then the work of the creative team is the heart and soul.

WEB ART DIRECTOR

When people who work in marketing and advertising talk about art, they are referring to the visual elements that go into a campaign. These include videos, photographs, artwork, illustrations, graphics, and designs. Overseeing the use of visual elements that are part of Internet marketing and advertising is the Web art director.

As with other types of directors, Web art directors have a vision for each one of their projects. They see a "big picture," which is made up of several smaller visual elements woven together with text. The end result must provide information, promote sales, and represent the client's brand, all while also being pleasing to the viewer's eye.

Web art directors are normally hired from within, meaning that graphic designers who already work for a company

Web art directors combine various visual elements to create an overall online style.

or agency are promoted and named art director after proving themselves at their design jobs.

WHAT THEY DO

Web art directors are responsible for the overall look of clients' Web sites, banner ads, sales e-mails, and videos. Their job is to find, create, and place images and designs that will cause viewers to take action, whether it's clicking through a Web site or pulling out their credit cards right then and there to purchase a product.

Making decisions is an everyday occurrence for these professionals. They approve or disapprove of graphics and illustrations created by Web designers, as well as the angles, lighting, and subject matter of photographs and videos. Even something as seemingly simple as choosing the colors or font style used in an online ad must pass inspection by the art director. In making his or her decisions, the Web art director must keep in mind that it is not enough for the artwork in a marketing or advertising campaign to be simply beautiful and pleasing to the eye. The visual aspects of such work also have to represent adequately the company's brand and support and complement the text in such a way that they help convey the message being presented to prospective clients.

Interacting closely with clients to get input on the look and feel of Web sites is also in the job description for Web art directors. These individuals supervise other members of the team who are working on the visual aspects of projects, such as Web designers. In fact, many Web art directors start out as Web designers, so it should come as no surprise that many of these professionals actively participate in the creation of artwork for a marketing piece themselves, rather than just supervising. Coordinating with other departments such as copywriting and production is another job duty. As the head of a department, Web art directors are also in charge of budgets for their entire department and for each project they undertake.

EDUCATION AND TRAINING

A bachelor's degree is pretty much a must for anyone who wants to work as a Web art director. Some combination of arts-focused and technology coursework would be best. For instance, the résumé of someone with a bachelor of arts (BA)

A love of art is essential for anyone striving to become a Web art director.

or bachelor of fine arts (BFA) degree in design who also had a minor or concentration in computer science would probably catch the attention of a company looking to hire a Web art director.

At the very least, Web art directors will need to know how to use the computer software programs most commonly used by designers. Many high schools and most colleges offer classes in which students use these programs regularly and become skilled in their use. Community education programs frequently offer courses in using specific programs, as do some stores that sell computers. Some companies even offer employees training that will keep them updated on the latest software to help them do their jobs well.

Obviously one of the most important skills a Web art director can have is the ability to know what looks good, which is sometimes known as a "good eye." This is not necessarily something that can be taught. However, the proper training and education can strengthen a person's abilities in this area. Art appreciation courses might be an option.

WHAT THE FUTURE HOLDS

Predicting the future of online art directors is difficult. The *Occupational Outlook Handbook* anticipates that, overall, jobs for art directors will grow slowly compared to other fields. Yet there is good news for those hoping to be art directors for advertising and marketing firms. There should be the most job openings for these positions. The trend toward digital advertising and marketing is also good news for individuals interested in this particular career. Art directors who are trained in online software programs and have experience working with digital media are expected to be in demand as more companies strengthen their Web presence.

Another consideration is competition for online art director jobs. Fewer new jobs for art directors overall because of slow growth in the field, and a shortage of traditional advertising and marketing positions means that more people will be applying for a dwindling number of jobs.

WEB DESIGNER

Online art directors have an overall vision of how a Web site should look, and some actually produce the visual elements that go on the site. Yet the bulk of creating a Web site's appearance is the duty of Web designers. In traditional advertising and marketing, the Web designer's counterpart is a graphic designer. The difference between the two lies in the programming Web designers need to do in order to make their sites function properly.

Mapping out the architecture of a Web page is a large part of what Web designers do.

WHAT THEY DO

Web designers do more than just find pretty pictures and stick them up on the Internet. Beyond making their work look good, designers must also keep in mind how the visuals and graphic elements they use function on the screen. The

INFORMATION ARCHITECTURE

Anyone who has ever surfed the Web understands that the Internet is filled with an enormous number of connections, which allow users to move from one site to another and within the many pages of an individual site. The organization that makes these connections work smoothly is called information architecture.

Much as traditional architecture starts with a blueprint, information architecture on the Web begins with a similar type of planning. Web developers and designers frequently use diagrams or page mockups, called "wireframes," to help them see where all the connections need to take place. Using these wireframes, Web developers then build a Web site by creating several individual pages (with the help of Web designers and copywriters, of course) and writing computer code that makes every button, drop-down menu, and link on those pages work properly.

The idea is to help users find information easily, with as few clicks of the mouse as possible. To do this, the people in charge of information architecture must anticipate how users will most likely use the site. Thinking like a user who is fresh to the site helps information architects decide where to place certain information and the onscreen devices that help users get where they need to go.

first step in designing a Web site is meeting with the client to see what his or her Web needs are. These meetings are usually held with other key members of the marketing team, especially the account executive and the online art director. Everyone needs to be in agreement about the look and usefulness of the site, including what kind of artwork best represents the clients and his or her product or service.

Next comes the layout. Web site designers must figure out how to best arrange all the elements that go on each electronic page of the site, even before they pick the specific graphics—visual elements such as photographs and illustrations—or have the copywriter's text in hand. They make sure that site pages are not overcrowded or messy so that viewers can find the information that they need and the client's sales message gets through as well.

At this point the architecture of the site, which controls how the information flows throughout the pages of a Web site, must also be considered. This involves the ability to write a certain amount of computer code, or at least the ability to operate programs that generate code. Large marketing departments or companies generally have a Web developer, also known as a Webmaster, handle tasks related to information architecture. In smaller marketing firms or operations, the Web designer might also act as an information architect.

Another duty of Web designers—the one most people automatically think of when they hear the job title—is to find or create the pictures, illustrations, and designs that are seen on each page of a Web site. Using a number of graphic design software programs, Web designers draw, place, clean up, and manipulate these graphic elements and flow in text to create a polished, effective Web site.

EDUCATION

People can start to train for a career as a Web designer in high school. Art classes can help hone people's artistic talents, and computer classes give them technical skills they will use later on the job. Students can put both of these things to good use while still studying by designing school publications or, more in keeping with the online aspect, offering to design the Web sites of school clubs.

Earning a bachelor's degree in design is a smart move as well. Many colleges offer degree programs where students not only learn the theory behind design but also get hands-on experience with a variety of software programs. Any college with a computer science program should offer undergraduate, and possibly graduate (master's), degree programs in graphic design. Aware that Internet marketing and advertising is a growing field, the faculty at these colleges make sure to add Web design to the curriculum. There are colleges and universities that specialize in graphic design, including Web design. These schools often will have the terms "art and design" or "graphic design" right in their names.

Many advertising and marketing firms prefer to hire people who have at least a couple years of college under their belts. Short of getting a four-year or even two-year college degree, however, someone hoping to get a job as a Web designer should, at the very least, take as many classes as possible on how to use design software programs. The programs these professionals use the most include Photoshop, InDesign, Illustrator, CorelDraw, and the like. Knowledge of basic HTML (hypertext markup language) and/or JavaScript is pretty essential as well.

Web designers should be proficient in using many different types of design programs.

WHAT THE FUTURE HOLDS

The job market for online graphic designers should remain strong as long as advertising and marketing is being conducted via the Internet. That's pretty good news for anyone looking to get a job in this field. Internet advertising and marketing accomplished through companies creating Web sites alone has grown quite a bit over the years. Considering growth in the introduction of new methods of delivering marketing messages, such as electronic versions of magazines and newspapers and devices such as smartphones, the outlook looks good for prospective online designers.

The news in this area that's not as good is that the competition for available jobs is expected to be fierce. Applicants with an advanced degree or, more important, experience designing Web sites should have the edge.

ONLINE COPYWRITER

Online copywriters are the people who write the words (copy) that appear in online advertisements and other digital marketing pieces. Web content managers are in charge of writing and placing the creative text that appears throughout Web sites and other online information portals, such as blogs and online chat pages.

WHAT THEY DO

Writing is a process that has several steps. Online copywriters typically start the process by conducting research into what they're writing about as well as information about the audience that will receive their marketing message. Copywriters must understand a product or service in order to explain what it is they're selling to prospective buyers. Part of their research, then, includes talking to the client, using the product or service themselves, and investigating what other similar items are already on the market. Researching the audience they're trying to reach helps online copywriters decide what tone their writing should take, as well as what parts of a product to emphasize, so they can tempt readers to become buyers.

The next step in the writing process involves coming up with ideas. Typically writers take part in brainstorming sessions with other team members working on a campaign.

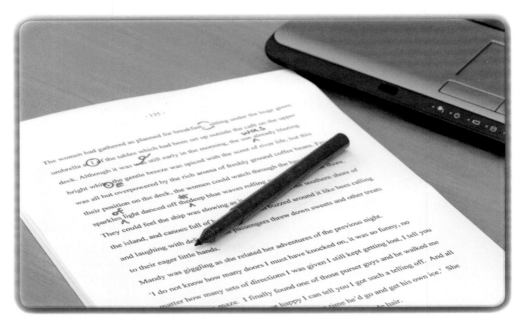

Copyediting has traditionally been done with pen and paper. However, more and more copy editors are doing their work online.

These sessions are a jumping-off point for writers, who then must come up with more ideas regarding themes and word choice that will best convey the campaign objectives. After a brainstorming session or two, writers then start to write drafts, which are early versions of the copy they plan to use. It is not unusual for advertising and marketing agencies to create multiple presentations for a single product or service. Drafts may be written by copywriting teams, but generally online copywriters work alone at this stage, particularly if they work for a small firm or department.

After final drafts have been written, copywriters then present their work to their bosses—either editors or the online art

ADVICE FROM A WEB CONTENT SPECIALIST

Richard is a freelance writer and blogger who specializes in personal finance and business matters. His work has appeared on the *Huffington Post* Web site and CNNMoney online. Before becoming a freelance writer, he spent more than twenty years as marketing director of an investment advisory firm.

Richard is "cautiously optimistic" when it comes to predicting the future of Internet marketing writing, including blogging. "The explosive growth of online marketing has done a great deal to make up for the decline in traditional writing jobs, such as with newspapers," he says. "However, online marketing is nearing a more mature phase of its development, where growth rates will be slower, and advertisers start to ask hard questions about which approaches are giving them a good return on investment.

"In short, there will continue to be a market for bloggers and digital copywriters, but it will be competitive. Writers will have to be good at engaging readers and communicating information thoroughly and succinctly, and they'll have to know their subject matter."

His advice for online copywriters and bloggers is to visit many different company Web sites and blogs to see what approaches others in the business take. Online marketing hopefuls should incorporate elements that seem to work well into their own writing. Likewise, they should avoid using techniques that seem to fall flat, are confusing, or just plain fail to get their message across to the reader.

"Be prepared to pay some dues," Richard says. "No one starts off as a high-profile blogger or as a well-paid online writer. However, if they do good work, they will build a reputation" that should attract employers and get them job offers.

director, or both—and, eventually, to the client. Usually two or three choices are presented to give the client options.

Writing that is to the point and brief is important in marketing and advertising. This is especially true of Internet advertising and marketing. Online copywriters need to be sure that their language is straightforward and concise, while still giving customers or Web site viewers plenty of information. Weaving in links, which Web designers will make active by inserting hypertext code, in such a way that the copy still reads smoothly and naturally is also the job of online copywriters.

Writing copy may be only part of what online copywriters are expected to do. Many also are required to keep track of the information on a client's Web site, updating and replacing content as needed.

EDUCATION

Obviously any class that involves writing would be helpful to someone who wants to become an online copywriter. Literature classes, which involve reading classic and modern stories, are also helpful, since they give students a "feel" for language and how good writing keeps a reader's attention. Taking social science courses such as psychology and sociology gives would-be online copywriters insight into the psyche of customers, and classes in business help prepare them for the work world.

English, journalism, and communications are good majors for prospective online copywriters to consider when they enroll in college. Computer classes give online copywriters a base of knowledge in the software programs used in advertising and marketing. While not all online copywriters are required to perform graphic design duties, some are—and extra knowledge about many aspects of Internet advertising and marketing is not a bad thing.

A track record of well-written reports and term papers is usually not enough to get someone a job as an online copywriter. Employers like to see that copywriters have firsthand experience writing for a variety of publications, both online and off. Therefore, gaining an internship with an advertising or marketing firm is an excellent source of on-the-job training. Gathering together writing samples completed during the internship in a professional portfolio is something prospective employers need to see in addition to a résumé.

WHAT THE FUTURE HOLDS

Because a writing career is considered by many people to be exciting and glamorous, getting a job as an online copywriter might be difficult due to the competition for such positions. At the very least, prospective employees can expect to compete with many other hopefuls for openings in this field.

Complicating the employment situation for those who want to be online copywriters is the fact that there are not as many writing jobs of any kind as there once were. Thanks to the rise in company Web sites and increased interest in advertising online, there is one sector that seems to hold promise for the foreseeable future—online writers. Copywriters with experience writing for the Web should be in demand as long as technology trends continue.

CHAPTER 4
Analysis and Outreach

The object of marketing is to sell products and services. To do that, companies need to attract new customers and keep old ones. Advertisers and marketers have two main tools that help them focus on customers: analysis and outreach.

Analysis involves examining data concerning the behavior of customers, to see how they shop and what types of items they are buying. That information can be used by marketers to target customers, increase sales, and determine how effective their current sales efforts are. The people who analyze Internet marketing data are search engine marketers, which include search engine optimization specialists, and Web analysts.

Outreach is a way to communicate with new and existing customers in a way that goes beyond simply trying to sell them something. When it comes to marketing, outreach is about making connections, sharing information, and creating goodwill. Online outreach is the responsibility of social media specialists.

SEARCH ENGINE MARKETER

The rise of Internet advertising and marketing has led to a number of new, Web-specific job titles. Among these is search engine marketer. People in this position specialize in using Internet search engines—computer programs that act as electronic indexes for information that can be found online—to

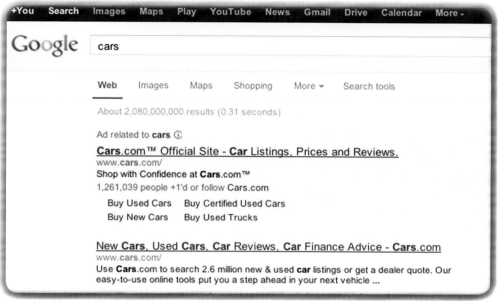

Ads selling cars appear on a Google (www.google.com) search engine Web page showing results from a search for the word "cars."

boost client visibility and sales. Popular search engines include Google, Yahoo!, and Bing.

Search engine marketers are similar to online account executives in that they run advertising and marketing campaigns for clients. The difference is that the former professionals are dealing with campaigns focused within the realms of search engines only.

WHAT THEY DO

Search engine marketers spend a large part of their day thinking up ways to get more traffic to their sites or those of their

SEARCH ENGINE MARKETING IN BRIEF

Search engine marketing can be either paid or what marketers call "organic" or "natural." In paid search engine marketing, companies bid on the right for their Web site to appear when a certain word or term connected to their company, called a keyword, is keyed into a search engine. Their appearance on a search site is in the form of an advertisement. The more money that is bid, the higher on the list of search results a company's ad ought to be. Organic search marketing involves placing keywords within a Web site that are relevant to the site's topic and are most likely to be used in a person's search. Organic search marketing is not connected to advertising, so it is free.

Search engines list their paid and organic results on the same pages. The ads tend to look like the organic listings, although paid search ads are typically set aside in some way. Some are separated from organic results by some type of graphic element (lines, boxes) and/or simply labeled as an ad.

clients. Their primary goal is to get the company name in front of as many people as possible by having it come up early and often in Web search results.

When it comes to paid search—also known as pay per click (PPC) advertising—search engine marketers bid on the rights to keywords and phrases that, when used during a search by potential customers, cause an advertisement linked to their Web site to appear on search index pages. Search engine vendors such as Google get paid the amount bid every time someone clicks on an ad.

Search engine marketers need to decide how much they are willing to pay the vendors every time a viewer clicks on the company's advertisement that appears in the search results. Considerations that affect this decision are their budget, as well as whether or not the company will make more money than it has to pay for total number of clicks for as long as they have a winning bid.

Organic search campaigns are handled by search engine marketers as well. When dealing with the latter, they may also be referred to as search engine optimization specialists. Search engine marketers specializing in search engine optimization decide what keywords will be used and their strategic placement on a Web site's pages. Places where it is most useful to place keywords are in the title and early on in the page's text. Sometimes it is enough to simply include keywords prominently on Web pages to get a hit. Often search engine marketers will take advantage of a page's HTML coding to have search engines call attention to a certain word or phrase. This is a process known as meta tagging. The purpose of all this is to rank high on the list of items that appear on a search results page. The higher the ranking, the more likely people are to click on the link to a company's Web site—and the more likely they are to buy the company's products.

If all that was required was to string a bunch of words on a Web page to get search engine hits, then the search engine optimizer's job would be easy. However, companies want customers to read the information on their sites. Search engine marketers must work with copywriters to incorporate keywords and linked text smoothly and seamlessly into the Web site's copy.

Using Web analytics (often with the help of Web analysts), search engine marketers track how effective their

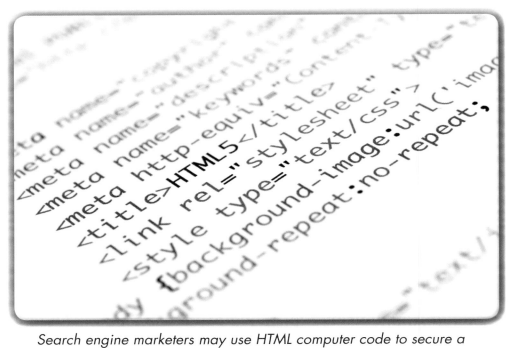

Search engine marketers may use HTML computer code to secure a high rank for clients' Web sites in a process known as meta tagging.

search strategy is. In an attempt to keep driving traffic to the sites they oversee, they refine and update their work on a continuing basis. Search engine marketers also encourage name-dropping, provided the name being dropped is their client's. In addition to strengthening the rank of Web sites on search results lists, they find ways to get their clients mentioned on other sites, blogs, and social networks.

EDUCATION AND TRAINING

High school and college students alike can prepare for a career as a search engine marketer by taking a wide array of classes in various disciplines, so that they come to their employers as well-rounded individuals. Of particular interest might be computer science classes, including courses that explore programming and data coding. Knowing the technology behind how search engines work is an advantage to prospective marketers. In addition, classes in psychology might help these individuals better understand the connections people make between keywords and the items they're searching for, and business courses provide a solid grounding no matter what career they pursue.

Some vocational schools and professional organizations offer certification in search engine marketing. Any information or experience in the field is helpful. The only cautionary note about certification is that standards for such courses, which determine what needs to be learned to earn certification, can vary among organizations.

It is wise not to overlook on-the-job training as well, which means learning about the field by performing the work. A 2008 report by the professional search engine marketing group SEMPO indicates that once a search engine marketer has gained at least five years of experience on the job, he or she gets a considerable bump in salary. Even work as an unpaid intern counts as experience.

WHAT THE FUTURE HOLDS

Search engine marketing is a relatively new career path, compared to jobs in traditional advertising and marketing or even their digital counterparts. Yet, as with other positions tied to the Internet, search engine marketing has been experiencing solid growth over the years. Professionals in this field are

ADVICE FROM AN ONLINE MEDIA MARKETER

Edton is a senior director of online media for the online marketing firm QuinStreet. In this position he oversees mostly the organic search engine marketing for the company and its clients. Originally employed by a traditional "offline" advertising agency, he made the switch to online marketing because of the immediate response he was able to get to his work.

While in high school, Edton was involved in a number of extracurricular activities that helped prepare him for his work in digital marketing. In addition to working on the student newspaper, he was heavily involved in a local chapter of the Future Business Leaders of America (FBLA), a national education association that prepares students for business careers. The

Members of the Future Business Leaders of America (FBLA) from Augusta, Georgia, prepare marketing materials promoting the organization.

newspaper gave him editorial skills, which he uses to write search-friendly copy, and involvement in the FBLA sharpened his organizational skills and gave him team leadership experience.

Edton suggests that anyone interested in the field of online advertising or marketing follow his lead and join extracurricular clubs and organizations that prepare individuals for the work world. He notes that Internet advertising and marketing employers are looking for workers who are well-rounded, "analytical as well as creative," and flexible, because things change quickly in the field. Beyond that, he highly recommends getting firsthand experience.

"Try to find a company to work with in order to immerse yourself in the online space, for example in the form of an internship," says Edton. "Don't get hung up on the specific aspect (search engine optimization, SEM, pay per click, etc.) since just breaking into one of these will be an entrée, and you'll likely be exposed to the other aspects and can explore them over time. You'll just learn so much by getting into it."

expected to be increasingly in demand as companies depend more and more on the Web for conducting business.

WEB ANALYST

Web analysts are essentially digital sleuths. They track customer visits to Web sites and analyze the data that they uncover, looking for patterns of use and buying trends. Discovering how visitors use a site provides Web analysts with clues regarding who is using the site, how they're using it, and how a site can be made more user-friendly and effective at selling.

Web analysts track the online behavior of people surfing the Internet to gain insight on popular trends.

In many ways the relatively new field of Web analytics is the digital equivalent of market research in traditional advertising and marketing. Market research analysts conduct surveys and polls. In addition to adapting such traditional methods for online use, Web analysts also have at their disposal sophisticated technology such as eye-tracking devices, which record the eye movements of Web site visitors, and heat mapping, which tracks how users navigate through a site by following the position of a user's computer mouse and where he or she clicks.

WHAT THEY DO

Web analysts review data that details how well Internet advertising and marketing campaigns are working. They crunch numbers and, based on those figures, decide what works on a Web site and what doesn't seem to work as well. They then recommend and institute changes to sites that capitalize on the good stuff and eliminate the less successful elements. They set goals regarding how well a Web site should perform, gauged by page hits and, ultimately, sales, then tweak sites to meet those goals. This typically is accomplished by changing and updating content on client sites.

To do their job, Web analysts typically use Web analytics software. However, working with Web developers, Web analysts might also create their own specialized data collection methods that are tailor-made to suit their purposes. No matter how it is collected, the information is still essentially raw data. Web analysts take that data and compile it into reports that are engaging and easy to understand. In their reports, Web analysts interpret their findings in such a way that they

Google Analytics (www.google.com/analytics) is a widely used tool for Internet marketers who specialize in Web analysis.

are able to offer constructive suggestions about how companies can fix trouble areas and build on their strengths.

Web analysts are also charged with keeping the information they gather secure. They must ensure that any information taken from a Web site—including private customer information such as credit card numbers—is not lost or used inappropriately. To help keep information safe, Web analysts usually set up a secure system for collecting the data, which may include special log-in procedures, passwords, and other methods for making sure that only authorized people have access to the information.

EDUCATION AND TRAINING

Employers seeking to hire a Web analyst would most likely look for someone who did well in a variety of subjects in high school. Of particular interest would be the grades someone received in math, since compiling statistics and figuring percentages are a daily occurrence in this job. An affinity for science classes might indicate to prospective employers that a student is familiar with observation and how to conduct research. A combination of information technology classes and marketing courses would be ideal for any college student looking to become a Web analyst.

There are organizations that offer certification in Web analysis and Web analytics, including the Digital Analytics Association. As with programs in search engine marketing, or any newer discipline, standards are not always set in stone. Therefore, certain aspects of being a Web analyst may not be covered as thoroughly as necessary for success in the field. However, when all is said and done, earning certification in Web analysis is a wise decision.

Web analysts need to be comfortable operating in the online environment. Some basic knowledge of jobs performed by others they work closely with, especially Web designers, is essential. Courses concerning how search engines work,

Web software programs, computer coding, and layout and design—taken either in school or through a community education program—would benefit someone hoping to become a Web analyst.

WHAT THE FUTURE HOLDS

The need for Web analysts is strong, as more and more companies are trying to optimize their overall online presence and give their Web sites a boost. The only drawback seems to be that smaller companies may add Web analytics to the workload of existing employees, such as those involved in Web site creation and maintenance. Larger companies, advertising agencies, and marketing firms are in a better position to make new hires regarding Web analytics—and even they may choose to consolidate Web analysis duties with other positions. Individuals willing to be flexible and perhaps start in a position dealing with Web oversight, even in a more clerical than professional capacity, stand the best chance of building a career in Web analysis.

SOCIAL MEDIA SPECIALIST

Social media sites such as Facebook, Google+, and Twitter can be a tremendous help in getting the word out about a company or product. Thanks to postings and the sharing of information among virtual friends, these types of networks are the electronic equivalent of old-fashioned word-of-mouth advertising. Hiring a dedicated, professional social media specialist is a move many companies are making in this increasingly high-tech age.

Social media specialists use such sites such as Google+, Facebook, and Twitter to spread marketing messages on behalf of their clients.

WHAT THEY DO

Imagine getting paid to chat online and create Web posts for a living. That's the general concept behind being a social media specialist. Rather than just posting about their day or expressing personal opinions, however, social media specialists deliver targeted messages in a very casual yet professional form.

Social media specialists are tasked with making sure client companies have a strong presence on social networking sites, blogs, podcasts, and other digital platforms. One way to do this is to have a business page on a social networking site such as Facebook or Yelp, complete with pictures and frequent updates. But just having a page where people can land isn't enough. Savvy social media specialists understand the give-and-take quality of such networking, forming a community of customer "friends" and "followers." Through social media pages they encourage customers to post a review, vote on an issue related to the product being sold, or repost text or video entries they find on the site. They offer coupons or other perks in exchange for customer information such as home or e-mail addresses and shopping habits.

Another tactic social media specialists use is creating a blog that discusses issues important to their company or their preferred customers. As a blogger, the social media specialist typically writes copy, finds images, and posts online content on a regular basis, whether it's weekly, daily, or several times a day. Content in a blog should revolve around professional concerns such as providing information on a product, announcing new ventures or community activities the company is undertaking, and discussing general topics within fields that affect the company and its customers.

EDUCATION AND TRAINING

As is true with any Internet advertising or marketing career, a well-rounded education, with an emphasis on math and computer science, is a definite plus for those working to become social media specialists. This field, however, is where firsthand experience can really pay off.

Obviously, many students have experience in creating Web pages on social networking sites and communicating on various electronic platforms—for their own personal use.

What they may not have, though, is experience blogging and sharing online with a business objective in mind. Anyone who wants to enter the digital career field as a social media specialist should consider blogging for a company or cause on a volunteer or internship basis.

WHAT THE FUTURE HOLDS

Millions of people around the world use social networking sites every day. That large a pool of possible customers can't be ignored. It makes sense, then, that social media specialists would be greatly in demand, so that they may reach out to all those customers. In a sense this is true—at least in regard to larger companies, which seem to be willing and able to invest in social media representation. According to a *Business Insider* article by Martin Zwilling, up to 47 percent of small businesses do not take advantage of social media for marketing purposes. Therefore, it's safe to predict that social media specialists will be part of overall growth in Internet advertising and marketing and could be even more significant as more small businesses hire for these positions.

CHAPTER 5

Digital Production and Media

In any Internet advertising or marketing effort, there are certain individuals whose job it is to support the "setup" of the account execs and creative people by working the nuts and bolts aspect of making a sale. These are the folks who manage the workflow so that deadlines are met, such as digital production managers. Other individuals in this category include media planners and media buyers—collectively known as online media specialists—who arrange to place ads and other marketing materials where the target audience is best able to find them.

DIGITAL PRODUCTION MANAGER

When thinking about what digital production managers do, it might be helpful to think of them as Internet advertising and marketing traffic police. They direct the flow of work traffic to make sure everything goes smoothly, offer direction when needed, and help enforce the business rules.

WHAT THEY DO

Digital advertising production managers work to put advertisements that promote clients' products online in any number of digital formats or media. These individuals also coordinate

Banner ads grace the Web sites of nearly all the major news organizations. Advertising revenue is a major part of their business model.

the work of other members of the online advertising team, such as Web designers and copywriters, during the preparation of such ads.

To help them accomplish their tasks, they prepare tables and schedules that outline who on the team is responsible for what duties, following specifications agreed to by all staff members, especially managers and directors, regarding how business should be accomplished within the company. Digital production managers then follow up with individual team members to see how the work is coming along and if there are any problem areas that need to be addressed.

Making sure that the team has everything it needs to complete the campaign is also part of a digital production manager's job description. These resources include anything from having the newest version of software available to assigning the right people—those who have the most experience with a particular client, product, or online medium—to the campaign. They also need to make sure everyone has current and accurate information about the campaign, alerting everyone to any changes in the schedule.

EDUCATION AND TRAINING

A bachelor's degree in marketing, advertising, or business helps prepare individuals for a career as a digital production manager. Experience with various scheduling and tracking software programs, which are used to create the schedules that are so important in this job, is important as well.

There are other aspects of the job for which the best training is experience. Online production managers are very detail and deadline oriented. They also need to be good communicators, since they are in constant contact with various team members. Completing an internship, either in an online production manager's office or in any advertising or marketing department, where one can learn time-management skills and the ability to coordinate the work of others, looks good on the résumé of a production management hopeful.

WHAT THE FUTURE HOLDS

As new media gains a bigger share of the advertising market, the demand for people with digital expertise will grow, which

Young people who are computer savvy have an advantage in the Internet advertising job market. Digital skills are an attractive credential to any company.

means more positions such as digital production manager should become open. Yet jobs in advertising and marketing are very popular, and digital production management is no exception. Expect strong competition for jobs of this nature. Furthermore, because this is a management position, employers will most likely look to hire someone with previous experience or someone within the company or firm who has worked for a few years at an entry-level position.

ONLINE MEDIA SPECIALIST

Successful online advertising campaigns don't happen by accident. A lot of thought goes into everything from the best words and images to capture an audience's attention to how much a product or service should cost, as well as what digital media should be used to make the best use of the campaign's other elements. Choosing what form of digital media is the right fit for a particular campaign, as far as visibility and cost-effectiveness are concerned, is the job of the online media planner. Purchasing space to run advertisements on specific digital formats, based on the online media planner's recommendations, is the job of the online media buyer.

WHAT THEY DO

Online media specialists use a specific knowledge set on the job that revolves around Internet usage by the typical consumer. Of course, the catch there is that who the "typical consumer" is changes with each product, service, and client. Therefore, these professionals make it their business to know as much as they can about the different types of digital media, what kinds of people are more likely to use each type of media, the various kinds of advertising that can be done online, and how much it costs to place advertisements with each online outlet.

Research is one key to being successful in this line of work. Much like Web analysts, who study data concerning how Web sites perform based on viewer usage, online media specialists analyze consumer habits as well. The only difference is that they do so before a campaign is set up, rather than after the launch. Online media planners create questionnaires and surveys—most of which are conducted online—that unlock basic yet important information regarding respondents. The answers people give to their questions help determine the age,

AFFILIATE MARKETING

Researching and buying advertising space on a Web site is not the only way companies can make sales through Internet channels. Businesses can increase their virtual workforce and their actual sales by participating in affiliate marketing.

In this type of marketing, companies, referred to as merchants, seek out other businesses or individuals (such as bloggers) with a Web presence, called publishers. Publishers have a connection to the product or service the merchant is selling. In other words, the two parties share the same target audience. Once that connection has been established, a deal is made to feature an ad or link to the merchant's products on the Web publisher's site. Publishers make money every time a purchase is made by customers using the ad/link that appears on their affiliate site.

The example most people use to demonstrate affiliate marketing is Amazon, which is a huge player in the affiliate marketing realm. Because it markets and sells a variety of products, Amazon has connections to many Web site publishers. Amazon is a popular online merchant, so publishers want to be affiliates in the hope that they can earn a percentage of Amazon's sales in the process. As a result, the Amazon logo and links to the Amazon site appear all over the Web.

sex, geographic location, interests, and buying habits of the client's ideal customer. Online media specialists then gather together many people who meet most or all of the same criteria as that ideal customer to make up their target audience.

EDUCATION AND TRAINING

At both the high school and college level, the classes that best help someone get ready for a career as an online media specialist cover a broad range of topics. Communications classes provide the written and verbal skills necessary when interacting with the public, either via surveys or face-to-face. Math courses give experience in crunching budget numbers, and business classes help students polish their professional demeanor. Obviously, coursework directly in advertising/marketing would be a definite plus.

Students with strong interpersonal skills are well-prepared to work as online media specialists.

All such classes are beneficial, but there's no substitute for firsthand experience. Those who want to carve out a career as an online media planner should not only be knowledgeable of the many digital programs and outlets there are for advertising but also have at least basic experience operating those programs. This can be accomplished either by hands-on learning in a classroom setting or by volunteering one's services for a club or group that needs these programs run.

The *Occupational Outlook Handbook* predicts that all types of media planning positions should see the number of available jobs in the field increase steadily for quite some time. The increased use of new media, such as social networking and other digital formats, is expected to create even more opportunities. As with other Internet advertising and marketing positions, the increased demand should be met with a surplus of candidates, so competition for openings will be great.

WHAT THE FUTURE HOLDS

The Internet has brought about plenty of changes in the way people communicate and interact with one another. The arrival and growth of this interactive technology also has altered the way many companies do business, from creating virtual storefronts to advertising and marketing their products online. Along with these changes has come a bounty of new and modified jobs that are Internet-specific.

Today's advertisers and marketers must know more than how to sell. In addition, they must be technology savvy to compete in the workplace. Their knowledge has to go beyond simply knowing how to operate a computer. Experience with coding and search functions, as well as the latest design and content management programs, will serve Internet advertisers and marketers well, no matter what specific job title they want to have.

While traditional forms of advertising and marketing still exist, and likely will be used well into the future, there's no turning back from the digital breakthroughs in these fields. Individuals who train for and gain experience in Internet advertising and marketing will be the ones who reap the most career benefits.

analytics The process of analyzing data to arrive at a logical conclusion.

banner ad A graphic image, combined with text, that appears on a Web site to advertise a product or service.

blog A Web journal that contains comments and observations written by someone either for personal use or as a means to promote a business.

brainstorming The practice of group problem solving wherein individuals contribute ideas for the group's consideration.

branding Marking a product, service, or company as a unique entity through the use of thematic, repetitive marketing.

browser A computer program capable of accessing sites or information on the Web.

campaign What advertising and marketing executives call the grouping together of various project work done on a client's behalf.

content management system A software program that helps organize and manage all of the content (images and text) that appears on a Web site.

hypertext A type of computer code that lets readers move from one electronic document to another by clicking on a link.

inbound marketing The practice of creating marketing materials that Internet users find using specialized searches they create themselves.

information architecture The way information is organized and connections are made within a Web site; a site's operations blueprint.

media The various forms through which messages are conveyed; plural of medium.

new media A term used to describe the various forms of electronic communication.

organic search The practice of placing keywords within a Web site that are relevant to the site's topic and are most likely to be used in an individual's search.

outbound marketing The practice of sending out marketing messages to a wide audience in the hope that random customers will get the message and buy the product.

QR code A type of barcode that can be scanned using smartphone technology to access multimedia marketing information.

search engine Computer software that enables users to search for information on the Web based on key words or phrases.

vendor A person or company that sells a products or service.

wireframes Diagrams or page mockups used by Web developers and designers to help them see where the connections are within a Web site.

American Advertising Federation
1101 Vermont Avenue NW, Suite 500
Washington, DC
20005-6306 (202) 898-0089
Web site: http://www.aaf.org
The American Advertising Federation educates members on
   the latest trends in technology, creativity, and marketing.
   Among the federation's numerous educational programs
   are the National Student Advertising Competition and
   summer ad camps for high school students, based in
   Chicago and Washington, D.C.

American Marketing Association
311 S. Wacker Drive, Suite 5800
Chicago, IL 60606
(312) 542-9000
Web site: http://www.marketingpower.com
Established in 1937, the American Marketing Association
   provides resources, tools, and training to marketing
   professionals around the globe. Traditional and digital
   publications, a resource library, conferences, and an
   online job board are some of the perks the association
   offers.

Association of Canadian Advertisers
95 St. Clair Avenue West, Suite 1103
Toronto, ON M4V 1N6
Canada

(800) 565-0109

Web site: http://www.acaweb.ca/en

The Association of Canadian Advertisers is a national advocacy group for marketing-communications professionals. The organization provides professional development courses, as well as publications and research within the field.

Canadian Marketing Association
1 Concorde Gate, Suite 607
Don Mills, ON M3C 3N6
Canada
(416) 391-2362

Web site: http://www.the-cma.org

One of the Canadian Marketing Association's offerings is its Digital Day Conference, an annual one-day digital marketing event filled with speakers, workshops, and panel discussions. The association also provides other conferences, as well as seminars, online courses, and an array of services for student members.

Digital Analytics Association
401 Edgewater Place, Suite 600
Wakefield, MA 01880
(781) 876-8933

Web site: http://www.digitalanalyticsassociation.org

The nonprofit Digital Analytics Association offers training and certification programs for Web analytics professionals.

Interactive Advertising Bureau
116 East 27th Street, 7th Floor

New York, NY 10016
(212) 380-4700
Web site: http://www.iab.net
The Interactive Advertising Bureau develops industry stan-
    dards, conducts research, and provides legal support for
    the online advertising industry. Its membership consists
    of digital advertising professionals around the world.

Marketing Research Association
1156 15th Street NW, Suite 302
Washington, DC 20005
(202) 800-2545
Web site: http://www.marketingresearch.org
The Marketing Research Association gives members and the
    general public educational opportunities, career guid-
    ance, and access to the latest information in the field of
    marketing research.

WEB SITES

Due to the changing nature of Internet links, Rosen Publishing
has developed an online list of Web sites related to the subject
of this book. This site is updated regularly. Please use this link
to access the list:

http://www.rosenlinks.com/CICT/Adver

For Further Reading

Aroms, Emmanuel. *How to Create a Social Media Marketing Plan* (Kindle ed.). Amazon Digital Services, 2012.

Campbell, Mark. *Adobe Photoshop and Photoshop Elements for Teens.* Boston, MA: Thomson Course Technology PTR, 2007.

Eley, Brandon, and Shayne Tilley. *Online Marketing Inside Out.* Collingwood, Australia: SitePoint Pty. Ltd., 2009.

Fox, Vanessa. *Marketing in the Age of Google: Your Online Strategy Is Your Business Strategy.* Hoboken, NJ: John Wiley & Sons, 2012.

Friedman, Jay M., and David Wolk. *30 Days to Digital Media Expertise* (Kindle ed.). Plano, TX: IvyPixel LLC, 2012.

Grewal, Dhruv, and Michael Levy. *Marketing.* New York, NY: McGraw-Hill, 2009.

Handley, Ann, and C. C. Chapman. *Content Rules: How to Create Killer Blogs, Podcasts, Videos, Ebooks, Webinars (and More) That Engage Customers and Ignite Your Business.* Hoboken, NJ: John Wiley & Sons, 2012.

Hensley, Laura. *Advertising Attack.* Mankato, MN: Heinemann-Raintree, 2010.

Hunter, Nick. *Social Networking: Big Business on Your Computer.* New York, NY: Gareth Stevens, 2012.

Kerpen, Dave. *Likeable Social Media: How to Delight Your Customers, Create an Irresistible Brand, and Be Generally Amazing on Facebook (and Other Social Networks).* New York, NY: McGraw-Hill, 2011.

Kumar, Bittu. *Marketing for Beginners: The Key Concepts and Steps for Young Executives* (Kindle ed.). Hyderabad, India: V&S Publishing, 2012.

Mathieson, Rick. *Branding Unbound: The Future of Advertising, Sales, and the Brand Experience in the Wireless Age.* New York, NY: AMACOM Books, 2007.

Reed, Jon. *Get Up to Speed with Online Marketing: How to Use Websites, Blogs, Social Networking and Much More.* Upper Saddle River, NJ: FT Press, 2012.

Robbs, Brett, and Deborah Morrison. *Idea Industry: How to Crack the Advertising Code.* New York, NY: One Club Publishing, 2008.

Ryan, Damian, and Calvin Jones. *The Best Digital Campaigns in the World: Mastering the Art of Customer Engagement.* Philadelphia, PA: Kogan Page Limited, 2012.

Ryan, Damian, and Calvin Jones. *Understanding Digital Marketing: Marketing Strategies for Engaging the Digital Generation.* Philadelphia, PA: Kogan Page Limited, 2012.

Selfridge, Benjamin, Peter Selfridge, and Jennifer Osburn. *A Teen Guide to Building Web Pages and Blogs.* Waco, TX: Prufrock Press, 2009.

Sostre, Peter, and Jennifer LeClaire. *Web Analytics for Dummies.* Indianapolis, IN: Wiley Publishing, 2007.

Story, Mark. *Starting Your Career as a Social Media Manager.* New York, NY: Skyhorse Publishing, 2012.

Bibliography

American Marketing Association. "Resource Library: Dictionary." Retrieved August 22, 2012 (http://www.marketingpower.com/_layouts/Dictionary.aspx).

Bly, Robert W. *The Online Copywriter's Handbook.* New York, NY: McGraw-Hill, 2002.

Education-Portal.com. "Advertising Director: Educational Summary for Becoming an Advertising or Marketing Director." Retrieved August 22, 2012 (http://education-portal.com).

Ferguson Publishing. *Careers in Focus: Advertising & Marketing.* New York, NY: Facts on File, 2004.

Field, Shelly. *Career Opportunities in Advertising and Public Relations.* New York, NY: Ferguson Publishing, 2007.

Franklin, Curt. "How Internet Search Engines Work." How Stuff Works. Retrieved September 24, 2012 (http://computer.howstuffworks.com/internet/basics/search-engine1.htm).

Internet World Stats. Retrieved July 29, 2012 (http://www.internetworldstats.com/stats.htm).

Lynch, Patrick J., and Sarah Horton. "Web Style Guide." 2011. Retrieved August 22, 2012 (http://webstyleguide.com).

Maier, Andrew. "Complete Beginner's Guide to Information Architecture." The UX Booth. Retrieved July 14, 2012 (http://www.uxbooth.com/blog/complete-beginners-guide-to-information-architecture).

Meerman Scott, David. *The New Rules of Marketing and PR.* Hoboken, NJ: John Wiley & Sons, 2009.

Newcomb, Kevin. "Search Marketing: A Rewarding Career Path." Search Engine Watch. Retrieved September 14, 2012 (http://searchenginewatch.com/article/2066811/Search-Marketing-A-Rewarding-Career-Path).

Princeton Review. "A Day in the Life of a Web Art Director." Retrieved August 22, 2012 (http://www.princetonreview.com).

Pryzyklenk, Garry. "Top 6 Skills of a Great Web Analyst." Search Engine Watch. Retrieved September 14, 2012 (http://searchenginewatch.com/article/2065210/Top-6-Skills-of-a-Great-Web-Analyst).

Ramos, Andreas, and Stephanie Cota. Search Engine Marketing. New York, NY: McGraw-Hill, 2009.

Raptopolous, Lilah. "How to Hire a Social Media Specialist." Inc. Online. Retrieved August 22, 2012 (http://www.inc.com/guides/2010/08/how-to-hire-a-social-media-specialist.html).

Service Canada. "Sales, Advertising, and Marketing Managers." Retrieved August 22, 2012 (http://www.servicecanada.gc.ca/eng/qc/job_futures/statistics/0611.shtml).

Steinberg, Margery. Opportunities in Marketing Careers. New York, NY: McGraw-Hill, 2006.

Ten Golden Rules.com. "Account Manager: Internet Marketing." Retrieved July 15, 2012 (http://www.tengoldenrules.com/job-account-manager.htm).

U.S. Bureau of Labor Statistics. Occupational Outlook Handbook. Retrieved July 16, 2012 (http://www.bls.gov/ooh).

Weber, Larry. Marketing to the Social Web: How Digital Customer Communities Build Your Business. Hoboken, NJ: John Wiley & Sons, 2008.

Index

ABOUT THE AUTHOR

Jeanne Nagle is a writer and editor based in upstate New York. She has written marketing copy for local businesses and universities, which has appeared online and in print. She is the author of several career books, including *Careers in Television* and *Choosing a Career as a Coach.*

PHOTO CREDITS

Cover (background), p. 1 © iStockphoto.com/Andrey Prokhorov; front cover (inset), pp. 20, 30 Yuri Arcurs/Shutterstock.com; pp. 4–5 Bloomberg/Getty Images; p. 8 Luis Santos/Shutterstock.com; p. 10 © iStockphoto.com/SpiffyJ; p. 13 Comstock/Thinkstock; p. 15 Dmitriy Shironosov/Shutterstock.com; p. 17 Monkey Business Images/Shutterstock.com; p. 23 Sean Justice/Stone/Getty Images; pp. 24, 48, 63 iStockphoto/Thinkstock; p. 27 AFP/Getty Images; p. 32 Andreas Kuehn/Taxi/Getty Images; p. 34 Oxford/E+/Getty Images; p. 38 © David Young-Wolff/PhotoEdit; p. 40 Pixsooz/Shutterstock.com; p. 45 Google and the Google logo are registered trademarks of Google Inc., used with permission; p. 51 © Augusta Chronicle/ZUMA Press; p. 52 wavebreakmedia ltd/Shutterstock.com; p. 54 © 2012 Google Inc. All rights reserved. Google Analytics™ is a trademark of Google Inc.; p. 57 © iStockphoto.com/franckreporter; p. 61 © iStockphoto.com/fazon1; pp. 66 Rido/Shutterstock.com; interior page border image © iStockphoto.com/Daniel Brunner; pp. 9, 18, 35, 41, 46, 50, 65 (text box background) © iStockphoto.com/Nicholas Belton.

Designer: Brian Garvey; Editor: Nicholas Croce;
Photo Researcher: Karen Huang